JUDI DENCH BIOGRAPHY

The Untold Story of Dame Judi Dench

Written by Stone Walker

Copyright ©2024 by Stone Walker

All rights reserved. No part of this book may be reproduced, distributed, or transmitted in any form or by any means, including photocopying, recording, or other electronic or mechanical methods, without the prior written permission of the publisher, except in the case of brief quotations embodied in critical reviews and certain other noncommercial uses permitted by copyright law.

This book is a work of nonfiction. The views and opinions expressed in this book are solely those of the author and do not necessarily reflect the official policy or position of any individual or entity mentioned. Every effort has been made to trace and credit the copyright holders of quoted or reprinted material.

TABLE OF CONTENTS

INTRODUCTION

ROOTS OF INSPIRATION

NURTURING TALENT

APPEARANCE ON STAGE

TRANSITION TO THE SILVER SCREEN

MASTERY OF CRAFT

THE LEGACY UNFOLDS

CONCLUSION

INTRODUCTION

Few names in the performing arts elicit as much respect and adoration as Dame Judi Dench. Throughout the course of a six-decade career, Dame Judi has become a theatrical and cinematic legend, enthralling audiences with her tremendous talent and uncompromising commitment to her craft.

We travel through the victories, difficulties, and sheer genius that have shaped Dame Judi Dench's remarkable career in this examination of her life and legacy.

Dame Judi was born on December 9, 1934, in the charming county of Yorkshire, England. Her upbringing in the area of gently sloping hills and charming villages would have a lasting influence on her creative instincts.

She was raised in a home that valued books and the arts, so she was exposed to the transformational power of performance and storytelling at a young age.

Supported by her family, Dame Judi's love of performing developed as she participated in regional theater productions and refined her craft through intense training.

Her early life set the framework for a career that would quickly propel her to stardom on the big screen and on stage.

Dame Judi's rise to fame was quick. She made her stage debut with the Old Vic Company in 1957 and gained recognition for her amazing acting flexibility and engaging stage presence very fast.

She brought life to a wide range of roles, from Shakespearean heroines to contemporary matriarchs, capturing both audiences and reviewers with her nuance and honesty.

Dame Judi's career changed course in the 1980s when she entered the film and television industries. She accepted the task with her usual enthusiasm, even if she had some misgivings about the medium. She went on to give a string of outstanding performances that cemented her place as one of Britain's most renowned actors.

From her Oscar-nominated performance in "Mrs. Brown" to her BAFTA-winning turn in "A Fine Romance," she never ceased to enchant audiences with her flawless talent and captivating screen presence.

Dame Judi Dench's influence is as strong and enduring as ever as her storied career moves into its sixth decade.

She has received a staggering number of honors and recognitions, such as an Academy Award, several BAFTAs, and multiple Olivier Awards.

She is regarded as a genuine icon of theater and film, inspiring countless artists with her undying enthusiasm and limitless talent.

Dame Judi Dench's life story is a monument to the transformational potential of art and the unwavering spirit of human endeavor.

She has persevered in her quest of perfection, leaving an enduring impression on the entertainment industry and enhancing the lives of innumerable people along the way, from her modest upbringing in Yorkshire to her rise to widespread recognition.

Let's honor the lasting impact of a genuine cultural icon as well as the accomplishments of a consummate artist as we consider her incredible journey.

ROOTS OF INSPIRATION

A trip to Yorkshire, England's gorgeous landscapes is where Dame Judi Dench's artistic career began. Dench was born on December 9, 1934, in the peaceful countryside of this illustrious county.

Her early years were woven together by the richness of rural life, with the undulating hills and lush valleys serving as a backdrop for the development of her artistic soul.

In the protective arms of her family, Dench grew up in a home where a deep love of the arts was the norm. Here, in the warmth of family ties, were sown the seeds of her future love.

Yorkshire's sleepy towns and charming villages were not only her childhood home, but also the rich ground that would nurture her creative passions.

Dench was surrounded by a world full with stories and magic from a young age. She was captivated by the whispery melodies of ageless ballads and the crackling flames of hearthside tales, which sparked a love affair with narrative power that would change the course of her life.

Nevertheless, despite the idyllic allure of her upbringing, Dench had difficulties during her formative years.

The ghost of World War II hung heavy, casting a shadow over the peaceful countryside and permanently altering the collective memory of the country.

But Dench never gave up in the face of difficulty; her resolute determination was a tribute to the courage and resilience her Yorkshire heritage had given her.

Dench's passion for the arts grew stronger as the effects of the war vanished from view.

She discovered comfort and inspiration in the plethora of human talent all around her, from the revered pages of classic literature to the moving tones of orchestral music.

Dame Judi Dench's voyage started in the heart of Yorkshire, with the calm murmur of streams and the subtle rustle of leaves.

She set off on the journey that would make her one of the most admired actors of her time right here, in this historic county.

And even though she would be traveling far from the serene settings of her childhood, Yorkshire's spirit would always be a part of her, providing her with courage and inspiration as she set off on the incredible voyage that lay ahead.

The modest boundaries of Dame Judi Dench's family home provided a rich environment for the extraordinary gifts that she possessed.

Nestled in an environment of artistic appreciation and intellectual inquiry, Dench's early years were marked by the rich tapestry of her surroundings and the profound influence of her family.

Her parents led this caring environment and provided Dench with the foundation of unfailing support and encouragement for her budding ambitions.

Their unwavering faith in her potential and their passionate commitment to nurturing her interests gave her the priceless platform on which she would go on to construct her remarkable career.

But the distinctive fabric of Dench's environment also played a role in shaping her artistic sensibility, not just her family's support.

Dench was surrounded by an inspiring atmosphere in the picturesque Yorkshire countryside, where the undulating hills and lush valleys unfolded in a symphony of natural beauty.

Every element of Dench's surroundings, from the rustling leaves that graced the ancient trees to the whispering winds that danced through the undulating fields, served as a blank canvas for her imagination to run wild.

Yorkshire's charming cities and bustling villages, with their rich histories and lively people, gave her a plethora of experiences to draw from for her artistic pursuits.

Nevertheless, there were difficulties in Dench's home life despite the idyllic beauty of her surroundings.

The turbulent events of World War II cast a shadow over the peaceful countryside, permanently altering the Dench home and influencing the country as a whole.

Dench's resilience was built against this backdrop of unpredictability and turmoil; her unflinching drive to follow her passions served as a light of hope in the face of hardship.

Dench found comfort and inspiration in her family's loving embrace and the enduring beauty of her surroundings as she faced the challenges of her formative years.

The roots of her extraordinary genius were planted in this furnace of love and creation, setting the stage for a career that would eventually transform British theater and film.

A pivotal moment of self-discovery occurred in the peaceful surroundings of Dame Judi Dench's early years, amidst the picturesque beauty of Yorkshire.

This experience would forever alter the course of her life and spark a passion for acting that would last a lifetime.

Ever since her early childhood, Dench has been enthralled with the captivating power of narratives, which have the ability to transport listeners to both actual and imaginary worlds.

Her passion for the performing arts was sparked by the mellifluous melodies of ageless ballads and the hushed tales of ancient literature, all of which were present in the sacred halls of her family home.

But the full scope of Dench's artistic calling did not become evident until she took the stage for the first time. She was cast in a local theater play and, as the limelight beckoned and the curtain lifted to show a universe full of limitless possibilities, she was overcome with a flurry of emotions. Nervous anticipation mixed with thrilling delight.

During that little instant, when Dench took on the role of a character brought to life by the magic of acting, she felt a deep sense of connection, an unfathomable bond with something bigger than herself.

She seemed to have unearthed a creative and strength-filled hidden resource that was just itching to be let loose on the world.

Dench's love of playing grew with each role that followed, driven by a deep-seated need to bring the many characters in her imagination to life as well as a never-ending quest for artistic brilliance.

She portrayed humorous foils as well as tragic heroines, and she embraced every job with an unshakable devotion to sincerity and fervor, creating a lasting impression on both reviewers and audiences.

Dench's desire to pursue a career in the performing arts became stronger as her passion for the stage did. She set out on a path that would finally bring her to the height of achievement, one that was filled with setbacks, difficulties, and profoundly self-discovering moments, all with the unshakable support of her family and the infinite encouragement of her mentors.

Dame Judi Dench discovered her genuine calling in the theater, a calling that would define not only her profession but also her essence as an artist.

And even though there would be many unknowns and challenges along the way, she would confront the future with a clear sense of purpose and a firm belief in the transformational power of narrative.

JUDI DENCH BIOGRAPHY

NURTURING TALENT

Dame Judi Dench's rise to prominence in the arts was not just the consequence of her natural ability but also of the careful development of her skill throughout her early years of training.

Dench developed her skills with a persistent pursuit of greatness in the hallowed halls of theatrical academia and under the tutelage of distinguished mentors, setting the stage for a career that would completely transform British theater and film.

Dench showed a remarkable flair for the dramatic arts from her very first performances; her uncommon blend of innate talent and unwavering will helped her stand out from other performers.

She was a rising star in the making, though, because of her never-ending curiosity and her unshakable dedication to her art.

Immersing herself in the rich tapestry of dramatic theory and practice, Dench undertook a rigorous course of study under the guidance of esteemed mentors and experienced instructors.

From Shakespeare's ageless lessons to the cutting-edge inventions of modern theater, she embraced every class with a passionate devotion and an insatiable curiosity, keen to take in every nuance and subtlety of the trade.

Apart from her academic training, Dench actively pursued chances to hone her abilities via hands-on experiences. She enthusiastically participated in neighborhood theater plays and community events, belying her age.

She explored her characters' minds more thoroughly with each job, delving into the depths of human emotion with a sensitivity and boldness that enthralled both critics and fans.

But what set Dench apart as a rising star wasn't just her technical skill; it was also her deep comprehension of the transformational potential of narrative.

She aimed to transcend the stage and into the hearts and minds of audiences worldwide by illuminating the human condition in all its complexity through her performances.

Dench's self-assurance and understanding of her own artistic individuality grew along with her schooling and repertory.

Equipped with an impressive toolkit of abilities and a deep respect for the industry, she set out on the next chapter of her life with a mission and a resolve to make a lasting impression on the theater and film industries.

During her training and formative years, Dame Judi Dench laid the groundwork for her legendary career. This foundation was characterized by her unwavering belief in the transformative power of storytelling, her unwavering commitment to excellence, and her boundless passion for the dramatic arts.

Dame Judi Dench discovered a test and refinement ground for her skills in addition to a stage to practice her profession within the close-knit community of her local theater.

As a young actress, Dench's journey took her from modest origins in the heart of Yorkshire to the busy theaters of London's West End. Along the way, she had a number of life-changing events on the local stage.

Dench found a real playground for artistic discovery in the colorful tapestry of community theater, where the lines between performer and audience were dissolved with electrifying intensity and originality had no limitations.

Dench was able to fully immerse herself in the rich tapestry of human experience in every performance, from small-scale black-box plays to large-scale outdoor extravaganzas, giving her characters a depth and authenticity that belied their years.

Dench brought her passion and steadfast devotion to perfection to every part she took on, using the knowledge she had gained during her early training years to bring the characters she played to life on stage.

She embodied a tangible feeling of honesty and vulnerability in every performance, whether she was playing funny foils or tragic heroines. Her radiant presence and compelling stage presence captivated both audiences and reviewers.

However, Dench's deep love for the transforming power of storytelling drove her to pursue her passion for the theater rather than only the joy of peer recognition or acclaim.

She aimed to shed light on the complexity of the human condition through her roles in regional theater plays, providing viewers with a portal into imagined and actual worlds and encouraging them to go on a path of self-awareness and empathy.

Dame Judi Dench discovered a community and a purpose in the crucible of regional theater productions. This group is united by a mutual appreciation of the dramatic arts and a shared dedication to artistic quality.

Dench's gifts blossomed in this supportive atmosphere, setting the stage for a career that would eventually change the face of British theater and film.

Lessons learnt on the local stage would continue to influence Dench's approach to performing as her popularity rose and her repertory grew, giving each new role a depth and sincerity that would ultimately come to define her iconic career.

Even though she would be traveling far from the charming theaters of her childhood, the sense of belonging and friendship she had formed during those early years would always be a part of her, giving her strength and inspiration as she began the next leg of her incredible journey.

Dame Judi Dench's career as an actress was characterized by an uncompromising dedication to mastering her craft and a dogged quest of greatness in the furnace of artistic refinement.

Dench's journey from her first steps into the performing arts to her spectacular rise to the top of the acting profession was marked by an unwavering commitment to perfecting the subtleties of her trade and expanding the parameters of her creative expression.

Dench's intense training program, which included a thorough study of dramatic theory, vocal technique, and physical expression, was essential to her growth as an actress.

She immersed herself in the rich tapestry of theatrical heritage under the direction of distinguished teachers and honored mentors, finding inspiration in the cutting-edge innovations of modernist theater as well as the eternal lessons of Shakespearean lyric.

But what set Dench apart as a rising star wasn't just her technical skill; it was also her deep awareness of human nature and her natural ability to inhabit the minds of her characters with a nuance and authenticity that wowed both critics and audiences.

She aimed to shed light on the intricacies of human emotion via her performances, giving viewers a glimpse into the private thoughts and emotions of her characters and encouraging them to go on a path of self-awareness and compassion.

Dench approached her work with an intense devotion to authenticity and a sincere dedication to each new play. She dug deep into her characters' psyches and tapped into her own emotional reserves to give life to the roles that filled her theatrical world.

She embodied a tangible feeling of honesty and vulnerability in every performance, whether she was playing funny foils or tragic heroines, bringing the audience into the play's universe and keeping them enthralled until the very end.

Apart from her official education, Dench actively pursued chances to hone her abilities with hands-on involvement in various theatrical works, encompassing genres such as comedy, drama, and modern.

She tackled every project she worked on with an exploratory and curious mindset, rising to the challenges of each new role with courage and an uncompromising dedication to artistic integrity.

Through the rigorous process of artistic development, Dame Judi Dench not only became the epitome of an actor whose limitless inventiveness and unflinching devotion to her craft continue to inspire both artists and audiences.

Even if her career as an actor has brought her widespread recognition, the spirit of inquiry and discovery that characterized her formative years is still very much present and drives her to push the limits of her craft and discover new avenues for artistic expression.

APPEARANCE ON STAGE

Dame Judi Dench's journey from budding actor to industry icon began when she was given the chance to become a member of the prestigious Old Vic Company, a landmark event in her creative career.

Dench began a life-changing adventure that would mold her career and establish her as one of Britain's most esteemed performers as she took her place among the esteemed group of actresses.

Dench saw the invitation to join the Old Vic Company as a confirmation of her developing talent as well as a unique chance to work with some of the most renowned performers of her generation and fully immerse herself in the rich fabric of theatrical tradition.

She developed her skill with a passionate devotion and an unyielding commitment to excellence under the direction of renowned directors and seasoned actors, taking inspiration from the ageless lessons of Shakespearean verse and the cutting-edge innovations of modernist theater.

Dench made her professional debut with the Old Vic Company, showcasing her amazing flexibility and commanding stage presence. Her radiant performance and magnetic stage presence captivated both spectators and reviewers. Her portrayal of tragic heroines and humorous foils were nuanced and effervescent, respectively.

Her ability to inhabit the psyche of her characters with a depth and authenticity that belied her age was unmatched.

But what made Dench a unique talent in the Old Vic Company wasn't just her skill or her presence on stage; it was also her deep appreciation for the transformational potential of narrative and her unwavering dedication to the study of the human condition.

She aimed to shed light on the intricacies of human emotion via her performances, giving viewers a glimpse into the private thoughts and emotions of her characters and encouraging them to go on a path of self-awareness and compassion.

Dench embraced her job with a spirit of exploration and wonder with every new production. She accepted the demands of every new part with bravery and an unflinching dedication to artistic integrity.

She made an enduring impression on both spectators and reviewers with her performances, whether they were on Broadway or the West End. She gave a tangible feeling of honesty and vulnerability to her roles.

Through the trials of the Old Vic Company, Dame Judi Dench proved herself to be not just the ideal actress but also a visionary artist, an inspiration to both artists and audiences with her limitless inventiveness and unflinching devotion to her work.

Even though she has received widespread praise for her acting career, the collaborative and exploratory spirit that characterized her early years with the Old Vic Company is still very much present and inspires her to push the boundaries of her craft and discover new avenues for artistic expression.

Dame Judi Dench's rise to fame was due to more than just her extraordinary talent; it was also a reflection of her extraordinary range as an actress.

Since joining the prestigious Old Vic Company in her early years and going on to achieve success on the global stage, Dench has been recognized and praised for her ability to embody a wide range of roles with unmatched grace, realism, and depth.

Dench's reputation as one of the most versatile actresses in Britain grew along with her star. She disregarded norms and expectations in every character she took on, showcasing an incredible range from sad heroines to humorous foils, from regal monarchs to regular women attempting to make sense of the complex human condition.

Shakespearean heroines like Ophelia, Juliet, and Lady Macbeth were all portrayed by Dench with a depth and authenticity that struck a chord with both critics and audiences.

Her portrayals of these classic characters were characterized by a tangible sense of vulnerability and sensitivity.

She gained a devoted fan base and solidified her reputation as a leading lady of the theater thanks to her command of the bard's lyrics and her ability to bring these classic roles to life.

But Dench's versatility was not limited to her classical roles; it also included her willingness to explore a broad variety of genres and styles.

She showed an unmatched ability to tailor her skills to suit the demands of any role, infusing each performance with a palpable sense of truth and authenticity, from her BAFTA-winning turn in the romantic comedy "A Fine Romance" to her Oscar-nominated performance in the historical drama "Mrs. Brown."

Dench's reputation as a versatile actress grew with every new honor and award, securing her place as one of the most esteemed and renowned artists of her generation.

She made a lasting impression on the theater and film industries by bringing a unique blend of talent, passion, and grace to every role she played, whether she was lighting up the Hollywood silver screen or the stages of London's West End.

Dame Judi Dench is a great example of the transformational potential of skill and dedication in the performing arts canon.

Her incredible variety and steadfast dedication to perfection have enthralled audiences all over the world, from her modest upbringing in Yorkshire to her rise to international recognition.

Even though she has achieved great success in her acting career, her reputation as a true artist and a visionary whose limitless inventiveness inspires both artists and audiences remains as bright and vital as ever.

A long list of iconic roles and standout performances throughout Dame Judi Dench's lengthy career attest to her unmatched talent and lasting influence on the theater and film industries.

Dench has captivated fans and reviewers alike with her dominating presence on stage and her fascinating performances on television, bringing a wide range of characters to life.

Shakespearean heroines, which she has portrayed with unmatched grace and realism, rank among her most famous parts.

Dencht's ability to give these classic characters depth, complexity, and emotional relevance has captivated audiences since her melancholic depiction of Ophelia in "Hamlet" and her radiant version of Lady Macbeth in "Macbeth."

Her performances in these iconic parts are nothing short of remarkable due to her command of the bard's rhyme and her deep comprehension of human nature.

But Dench's influence extends beyond the world of classical theater. She has embraced a variety of genres and techniques across her career, giving each character a strong feeling of sincerity and reality.

She won an Academy Award for Best Supporting Actress for her depiction of Queen Elizabeth I in the romantic comedy "Shakespeare in Love," where she enchanted the audience.

Her portrayal of a woman looking for her long-lost son in the historical drama "Philomena" brought the audience to tears, and she was nominated for another Academy Award for Best Actress.

A beloved fixture in living rooms worldwide, Dench's ability to inhabit characters with depth and authenticity, coupled with her undeniable charisma and screen presence, has earned her critical acclaim for her work in television dramas like "A Fine Romance" and "As Time Goes By."

In addition to her work on stage and screen, Dench has also distinguished herself as a master of the small screen.

Dench's reputation as one of the most admired and revered actresses of her generation is only going to grow as her career develops.

She confirms her standing as a true artist with every new role, a visionary whose limitless inventiveness and uncompromising devotion to her work inspire both artists and audiences.

Even though she has achieved great success in her acting career, her legacy as a genuine icon, a lighthouse of brilliance in a world that is always changing, remains as strong and relevant as ever.

TRANSITION TO THE SILVER SCREEN

Much with many of the greatest theater actors of her century, Dame Judi Dench's entry into the film and television industries was first greeted with some skepticism, despite her commanding presence on stage.

Dench, who was used to the closeness and immediate nature of live performances, was worried about the screen's seeming limitations because she thought the subtleties of her work may be lost in the conversion to celluloid.

For Dench, moving from the stage to the screen was a step away from familiar ground and into unknown territory that was tinged with fear and uncertainty.

She was used to the intense intensity of the theater and wondered if the more nuanced aspects of her performances would translate to the more muted mediums of cinema and television, where every emotion and every soft spoken word was captured by the camera's unblinking eye.

Nevertheless, Dench welcomed the chance to broaden her creative horizons and experiment with new forms of expression, and she met the challenge of film and television with her customary grace and dedication.

She refined her skills with an uncompromising devotion to perfection and a relentless drive to suiting the needs of the medium with each new job.

During her initial ventures into film and television, Dench showed an exceptional adaptability and a natural comprehension of the distinct requirements of the media.

She wowed audiences with her captivating screen presence and flawless talent in everything from her breakthrough role in the BBC television series "A Fine Romance" to her critically acclaimed performance in the film adaptation of "A Room with a View," winning awards and recognition for her contributions to the film industry.

Dench's confidence and willingness to take chances increased along with her level of comfort with the medium.

She pushed the envelope of her craft with every new role, delving into uncharted emotional and character territory with a sensitivity and bravery that enthralled both reviewers and fans.

Through the trials of film and television, Dame Judi Dench not only proved to be an exceptional actor but also a true trailblazer, embracing new difficulties and pushing the boundaries of her profession to create a lasting impact on the entertainment industry.

Even though she had some early misgivings and doubts about making the transition from the stage to the screen, it turned out to be a life-changing event that enhanced her artistic abilities and opened up new opportunities for her that she could never have predicted.

A string of breakthrough roles that marked Dame Judi Dench's departure from the theater and brought her worldwide reputation as one of Britain's most respected actors, along with critical acclaim, were interspersed with her stage career.

Dench's radiant appearance and captivating screen charisma left an enduring impression on both audiences and reviewers with every new performance that she gave.

Queen Victoria was one of Dench's first major roles, appearing in the engrossing historical drama "Mrs. Brown" in 1997.

Dench portrayed the iconic monarch with a depth and authenticity that won her critical acclaim and her first Academy Award nomination for Best Actress.

Her portrayal of Queen Victoria as a heartbroken widow attempting to navigate the complicated relationships between power and love demonstrated her extraordinary range as an actor and solidified her reputation as a force to be reckoned with in the film industry.

After her breakthrough role in "Mrs. Brown," Dench wowed crowds once more with a string of outstanding performances that cemented her place among the greatest performers in Britain.

She received acclaim for her portrayal of the steely-eyed spymaster with a golden heart as M, the head of MI6, in the James Bond film series, giving the character a greater gravitas and elegance.

Her charismatic on-screen persona and her rapport with co-star Daniel Craig gave the venerable spy series a fresh perspective, gaining her a devoted following and solidifying her place as a revered cultural icon.

Apart from her cinematic endeavors, Dench garnered praise from critics for her roles in television dramas like "Cranford" and "The Last of the Blonde Bombshells."

Her capacity to embody characters with nuance and genuineness, in conjunction with her indisputable charm and on-screen persona, rendered her a cherished presence in living rooms worldwide, garnering a devoted fan base and bolstering her standing as one of the most esteemed actresses in Britain.

Dench's legacy as a true artist whose limitless imagination and unflinching dedication to her craft continue to inspire audiences and artists alike grew along with her career.

Even though she had some early misgivings and doubts about making the transition from the stage to the screen, it turned out to be a life-changing event that enhanced her artistic abilities and opened up new opportunities for her that she could never have predicted.

Not only can Dame Judi Dench play a wide range of characters, but she also adapts to various media and performing styles with ease, demonstrating her extraordinary versatility as an actress.

Dench has shown an amazing capacity to flourish in a wide range of artistic surroundings, from the revered stages of London's West End to the glamorous world of Hollywood, capturing audiences with her radiant presence and irresistible screen charisma.

The key to Dench's versatility across a range of media and aesthetics is her unfailing dedication to artistic integrity and her readiness to take on new tasks with poise and resolve.

She takes a curious and exploratory approach to every job, ready to push the limits of her skill and discover new forms of artistic expression, whether she's performing in the cramped quarters of a black-box theater or in the bright light of a large soundstage.

Dench's ability to adjust to the demands of the film during her move from the stage to the screen was quite extraordinary.

She was excited and nervous at the same time to explore the different potential and challenges that each medium brought, having become accustomed to the closeness and immediate nature of live performances.

Dench showed a remarkable versatility and an inherent awareness of the intricacies of film acting in her roles ranging from her breakthrough performance in the historical drama "Mrs. Brown" to her renowned depiction of M in the James Bond franchise.

She became a natural for the world of film and television because of her ability to portray complicated emotions with subtlety and nuance, as well as her compelling screen presence and exquisite timing. She received critical praise and became well-known as one of Britain's most respected actors.

Dench's versatility as an actor has been showcased by her performances in a diverse range of theatrical styles and genres, in addition to her work on cinema.

She has accepted the difficulties of every new role with a bold attitude and an unrelenting devotion to excellence, from classic Shakespearean dramas to modern comedies, and she has won honors and prizes for her services to the theater and film industries.

Dench's reputation as an artist whose limitless imagination and unrelenting commitment to her craft continue to inspire audiences and artists alike evolves along with her career.

Even though she had to adapt and evolve throughout her transition from the stage to the film, her unwavering commitment to artistic excellence is still very much alive and well, inspiring her to push the bounds of her skill and discover new avenues for artistic expression.

MASTERY OF CRAFT

A tribute to her great talent and limitless variety as an actress, Dame Judi Dench's artistic prowess is evident in her amazing versatility across a multitude of genres and personalities.

With unmatched grace and brilliance, Dench has spanned the entire canvas of dramatic expression, from the depths of Shakespearean tragedy to the heights of comedy wit. Her transforming performances have captivated both audiences and critics.

Dench's natural ability to inhabit a wide range of characters with depth, sincerity, and emotional resonance is at the core of her versatility.

She provides a tangible feeling of truth and humanity to every role, whether she is playing regal monarchs or regular people struggling with the challenges of daily life. This allows audiences to relate to her characters deeply and personally.

Shakespeare's most famous heroines have never looked better because to Dench's mastery of the bard's lyrics in the world of classical theater. She has given these characters a depth and subtlety that is just amazing.

Her ability to skillfully and authentically negotiate the complexity of Shakespearean drama has captivated audiences, whether she is playing Lady Macbeth's tragic intensity or Beatrice's humorous genius in "Much Ado About Nothing."

Still, Dench's abilities are not limited to classical theater. She has embraced a broad variety of genres and styles across her successful career, including historical dramas, romantic comedies, period plays, and modern thrillers.

She is keen to push the limits of her skill and discover new forms of artistic expression, and she approaches each new project with an air of wonder and investigation.

Dench received yet another Academy Award nomination for Best Actress for her outstanding performance as a lonely schoolteacher driven by obsession and envy in the critically praised movie "Notes on a Scandal."

She showcased her versatility and ability as an actress in the whimsical comedy "The Best Exotic Marigold Hotel," when she played a retired widow going on a new adventure in India, captivating audiences.

Dench's reputation as one of the most admired and respected actors in Britain is only going to grow as her career grows.

She confirms her standing as a true artist with every new role, a visionary whose limitless inventiveness and uncompromising devotion to her work inspire both artists and audiences.

Even if her journey has brought her widespread recognition, her unwavering commitment to artistic excellence is still very much alive and strong, inspiring her to push the limits of her craft and discover new avenues for artistic expression.

A diverse range of partnerships with renowned directors and co-stars have molded Dame Judi Dench's remarkable career, each of which has advanced her artistic development as an actress and enhanced the theater and film industries.

Dench has had the honor of working with some of the most renowned and esteemed artists in the business, from innovative auteurs to seasoned veterans.

Together, they have forged strong bonds and produced unforgettable performances that have made a lasting impression on both critics and audiences.

Dench's resolute dedication to the director's vision and her dynamic interactions with fellow performers are fundamental to her collaborative process.

She approaches every project with an attitude of openness and receptivity, eager to explore the creative possibilities that result from the synergy of collective skill and shared artistic vision, whether she is working with longstanding collaborators or forming new ones.

Over the course of her career, Dench has worked with a wide range of filmmakers, each of whom brought a distinct viewpoint and sensibility to the creative process.

She has embraced the chance to work with directors that challenge and inspire her, pushing her to explore new depths of character and emotion with each new part. From the careful craftsmanship of Kenneth Branagh to the audacious experimentation of Stephen Frears.

Dench has had the honor of working with a variety of renowned co-stars, each of whom has contributed their unique skills and perspectives, in addition to her partnerships with directors.

She approaches every new collaboration with a sense of respect and adoration, acknowledging the worth of the collective ensemble in bringing a story to life, whether they are established veterans or emerging talents.

In the critically acclaimed movie "Shakespeare in Love," Dench starred alongside a gifted group of co-stars that included Geoffrey Rush, Gwyneth Paltrow, and Joseph Fiennes. Each of them added a distinct element to the film's diverse array of characters.

She had a strong relationship with co-star Daniel Craig in the James Bond series, adding a tangible tension and intensity to their moments together.

Dench's reputation as one of the most admired and respected actors in Britain is only going to grow as her career grows.

She confirms her reputation as a true artist with every new project; she is a visionary whose limitless imagination and unshakable dedication to her work never cease to amaze audiences and fellow artists.

Even though her journey has brought her widespread recognition, she has never wavered in her commitment to teamwork and artistic excellence, which inspires her to push the limits of her craft and discover new avenues for artistic expression.

Throughout her long career, Dame Judi Dench has consistently pushed the boundaries of her trade and pursued artistic greatness. Her career is a monument to the development of her acting style and technique.

Dench's approach to acting has changed dramatically over the course of her career, from her early days as a young actress in Yorkshire to her successes on the Hollywood and West End stages.

These experiences and a wide range of other influences have enhanced her artistry and broadened her understanding of human nature.

Dench's career as an actress has been driven by her uncompromising commitment to character and emotional development.

Using a diverse range of dramatic theory and technique, she has refined her craft with an unwavering dedication to genuineness and an adventurous attitude of trying new things.

She has embraced a wide range of inspirations, from the avant-garde innovations of Method acting to the classical teachings of Stanislavski, and combined them into a distinct and intensely personal style of performance that is both engaging and dynamic.

Dench's acting has always been distinguished by a unique blend of emotional nuance and technical dexterity.

She embodies a tangible feeling of truth and vulnerability in every role, whether she's playing funny foils or tragic heroines, and she immerses herself in her characters' minds with an intensity and fearlessness that enthralls both reviewers and spectators.

Her flawless timing, skill, and ability to delicately and nuanced portray complicated emotions have made her a true powerhouse on stage and cinema.

Dench's acting style has developed along with her career, growing and changing to suit the needs of every new part and media.

She has embraced the special chances and challenges offered by each medium, from the cramped quarters of the stage to the vast expanses of the silver screen, pushing herself to discover new emotional and character depths with every new endeavor.

Dench's acting has become more nuanced and mature in recent years, a reflection of her lifetime of dedication to the art as well as her wisdom and experience.

She reinvents her approach to acting with a spirit of inquiry and discovery that is as inspiring as it is admirable, pushing herself and expectations with each new part.

Dame Judi Dench is a great example of the transformational potential of skill and dedication in the performing arts canon.

Her incredible variety and steadfast dedication to perfection have enthralled audiences all over the world, from her modest upbringing in Yorkshire to her rise to international recognition.

Even though she has seen development and change in her career as an actress, her unwavering commitment to the profession of acting is still strong and alive, inspiring her to push the bounds of her skill and discover new avenues for artistic expression.

THE LEGACY UNFOLDS

Numerous honors and recognitions have dotted Dame Judi Dench's distinguished career, attesting to her unmatched brilliance, unwavering commitment, and enduring achievements to the theater and film industries.

Dench's mantel is adorned with a glittering array of acknowledgment that speaks to the tremendous effect of her craft and the enduring impression she has left on the cultural landscape, from major honors granted by prominent institutions to gushing praise from critics and viewers alike.

The highest distinctions in the entertainment industry, including as many Academy Award nominations and wins, Golden Globe Awards, BAFTA Awards, and Screen Actors Guild Awards, are the crowning achievement of Dench's career.

These much-desired awards are proof of Dench's tremendous talent and the praise she has received from critics for her ground-breaking stage and cinema roles.

Her portrayal of Queen Elizabeth I in "Mrs. Brown" and her Academy Award wins for Best Supporting Actress for "Shakespeare in Love" are among her most illustrious accomplishments.

These awards mark the apex of Dench's career and serve as enduring testaments to her extraordinary talent and enduring legacy.

Apart from her personal achievements, Dench has been honored by prestigious institutions and organizations worldwide for her services to the arts community. She has been granted honorary degrees, knighthoods, and lifetime achievement awards.

These accolades provide witness to Dench's lasting influence on culture and her status as one of the most venerated and well-respected actors of her time.

The industry's peers and colleagues, however, are the ones who have acknowledged Dench's ability and achievements arguably most meaningfully.

Actors, directors, and other industry professionals have praised her for her unmatched talent, professionalism, and generosity of spirit throughout her career.

The devotion and respect Dench commands from those who have had the pleasure of working with her speak volumes about her impact on the entertainment business, from glowing tributes at award ceremonies to poignant testimonies in interviews and press conferences.

A true legend whose extraordinary talent, commitment, and accomplishments continue to enhance the theater and film industries, Dame Judi Dench is remembered for her artistic brilliance and inspiration in the annals of performing arts.

Even though she has received innumerable honors and decorations for her achievements, her lasting legacy as a celebrated cultural icon and consummate artist is what really distinguishes her and guarantees her place in the pantheon of entertainment luminaries.

Dame Judi Dench's influence on the entertainment industry is immense, extending beyond the realms of theater and cinema to have a lasting impression on society.

Over the course of her more than 60-year career, Dench has enthralled audiences all over the world with her extraordinary talent, unshakable commitment to her craft, and timeless contributions to the storytelling genre.

Her unmatched ability to embody a wide range of roles with nuance, realism, and emotional resonance lies at the core of Dench's influence.

She infuses every role from Shakespearean heroines to contemporary matriarchs with an unmistakable feeling of truth and humanity, enabling viewers to relate to her characters deeply and personally.

Dench has elucidated the intricacies of the human condition via her performances, questioning norms and simultaneously arousing empathy.

In addition to her remarkable performances, Dench has been instrumental in changing the direction of British theater and film.

She has supported classical theater and honed the skills of future generations of actors and actresses as a founding member of the Royal

Shakespeare Company and a mainstay of London's West End.

Dench has contributed to the maintenance of British theater's vibrant history and sustained appeal for future generations by serving as a mentor and role model.

Dench's influence in the cinema industry has been similarly significant, since her remarkable skill and imposing presence on screen elevate the medium.

Her representations of strong, multifaceted female characters have broken preconceptions and altered the position of women in film, from her breakthrough performance in "Mrs. Brown" to her renowned role as M in the James Bond franchise.

Dench has questioned norms and prompted viewers to reconsider how they view gender and power in the entertainment industry through her performances.

However, Dench's motivation and influence over young performers and artists worldwide may be her greatest legacy.

Dench has been an inspiration to innumerable others who want to follow their hobbies and reach their creative potential because of her uncompromising devotion to quality, her steadfast devotion to her trade, and her ceaseless support of the arts.

Her legacy includes the dreams and lives she has inspired, in addition to her many honors and achievements.

Dame Judi Dench is regarded as a true icon in the annals of entertainment history, a visionary whose inexhaustible inventiveness, unshakeable morality, and enduring achievements keep the theater and film industries vibrant.

Even if her career as an actor may have come to an end, her influence on culture will live on for many generations to come, which is proof of the ability of art to inspire the human spirit, break down barriers, and question norms.

Dame Judi Dench will continue to affect the performing arts for years to come, and her impact on upcoming generations of actors will be felt long after her own distinguished career has ended.

Being a trailblazer in the theater and cinema industries, Dench has inspired and modeled herself for young actors worldwide, sharing priceless knowledge about artistry, professionalism, and the quest of greatness.

Dench's unflinching commitment to her profession and her unrelenting pursuit of artistic integrity are at the core of her influence.

She has proved the power of acting as a means of self-expression and storytelling via her transformational performances and her dedication to authenticity, motivating many people to follow their passions and aim for greatness in their own artistic pursuits.

Dench's impact extends beyond her creative accomplishments to include her support of up-and-coming artists and advocacy for the arts.

She has supported theater education and outreach initiatives wholeheartedly throughout her career, mentoring and advising budding actors and actresses from all backgrounds.

She has made it possible for the upcoming generation of artists to flourish and be successful in the cutthroat entertainment industry by her leadership and generosity.

Dench has broken down barriers and increased opportunities for women in the acting industry with her ground-breaking roles and unwavering support of the arts.

She has cleared the path for upcoming generations of female performers to take their proper position on stage and film, encouraging them to defy expectations and follow their ambitions with bravery and tenacity. She is one of the most admired and regarded actors of her generation.

However, Dench's most significant impact may come from the example she offers in her own life and career, which is proof of the strength of skill, diligence, and willpower in the pursuit of artistic greatness.

Aspiring actors and actresses have learned from her unshakable devotion to her craft that success is not only determined by plaudits and prizes but also by the impact we have on people's lives and the legacy we leave behind.

A visionary whose limitless inventiveness, steadfast integrity, and enduring achievements continue to inspire future generations of actors and actresses to dream big, work hard, and never stop striving for the stars, Dame Judi Dench is a true icon in the annals of performing arts.

Even though her career as an actor may have come to an end, her impact on the entertainment industry will live on for many generations, which is proof of the transformational power of art to mold minds, hearts, and souls.

CONCLUSION

The name Dame Judi Dench carries a resounding echo of greatness, grace, and unwavering spirit throughout the annals of theatrical history.

Over the course of a career spanning more than 60 years, Dench has dazzled audiences on stage and television with her unmatched talent, making a lasting impression on global culture.

Dench's career, which took her from modest Yorkshire beginnings to the pinnacles of international renown, is proof of the transformational power of talent, perseverance, and uncompromising commitment to craft.

She has defied expectations, dispelled myths, and expanded the definition of what it means to be an actor in the contemporary era with each new job.

Beyond the honors and recognition, however, Dench leaves behind an inspirational legacy that serves as a ray of hope for young performers and actresses everywhere.

She has made a significant contribution to the world of creative expression and activism by her ceaseless support of young artists and the arts, regardless of their upbringing or circumstances.

We are reminded of the ability of art to transcend barriers, bring people together, and inspire greatness as we consider the extraordinary career of Dame Judi Dench.

Her legacy will live on for many years to come, serving as a tribute to the strength of talent, perseverance, and the human spirit.

Shakespeare once said, "All the world's a stage, and all the men and women merely players." William Shakespeare's timeless verse has been brought to life by Dench's brilliant performances.

And in this grand theater of life, Dame Judi Dench has taken center stage, captivating audiences with her brilliance, touching hearts with her humanity, and leaving an enduring mark on the entertainment industry.

Printed in Great Britain
by Amazon